"It's so comforting to have a small piece of cake. Just one slice."

Mary Berry

i-Spark

i-spark.co.uk

PIECE OF CAKE

The Four Times Table in Story and Rhyme

Tracy Gillett Jo Horne

The baker's been busy, she's made lots of cakes,
but 40 gingerbread people have escaped.
Search through the pages and count as you find,
where they are hiding, with none left behind!

The baker's shop is the perfect place
to choose cakes, tarts and pies.
Watch as the customers choose their treats
and count how many they buy.

It's 8 a.m. and the shop is full
of wonderful goodies to eat.
Ting-a-ling-ling, someone's come in,
wanting to buy a sweet treat.

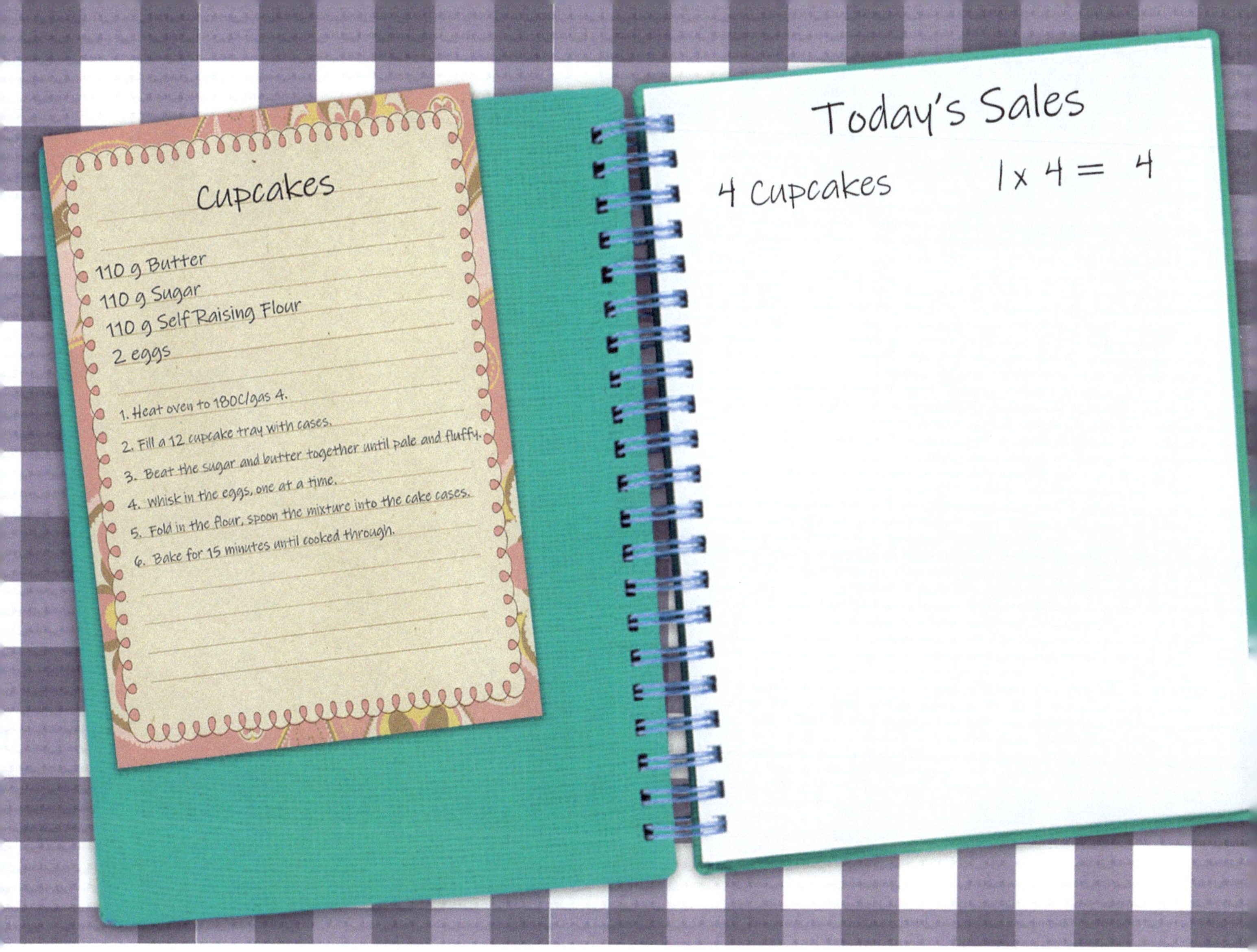

The builder would like 4 cupcakes
and he'll fix the squeaky floor.
The baker smiles, pops 4 in a box
and writes 1 times 4 is 4.

It's 9 a.m. and the shop is full
of wonderful goodies to eat.
Ting-a-ling-ling, someone's come in
wanting to buy a sweet treat.

The postie would like 4 crumbly cookies,
those that she's seen on the plate.
The baker grins, pops 4 in a box
and writes 2 times 4 is 8.

It's 10 a.m. and the shop is full
of wonderful goodies to eat.
Ting-a-ling-ling, someone's come in,
wanting to buy a sweet treat.

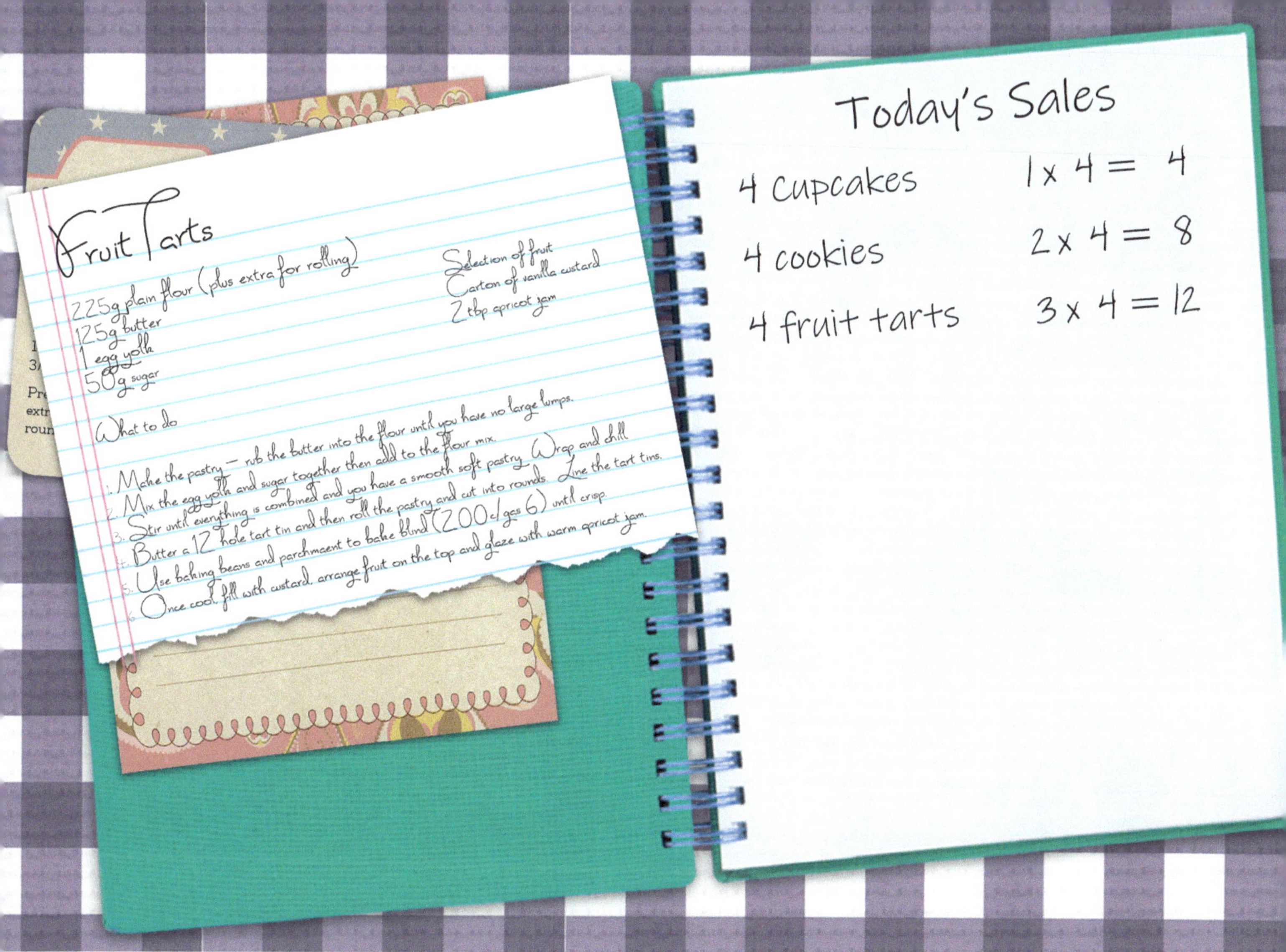

The nurse would like 4 fruit tarts,
"Do they taste as good as they smell?"
The baker nods, pops 4 in a box
and writes 3 times 4 is 12.

It's 11 a.m. and the shop is full
of wonderful goodies to eat.
Ting-a-ling-ling, someone's come in,
wanting to buy a sweet treat.

The doctor would like 4 apple pies,
the 4 through the window she's seen.
The baker agrees, pops 4 in a box
and writes 4 x 4 is 16.

It's 12 noon and the shop is full
of wonderful goodies to eat.
Ting-a-ling-ling, someone's come in,
wanting to buy a sweet treat.

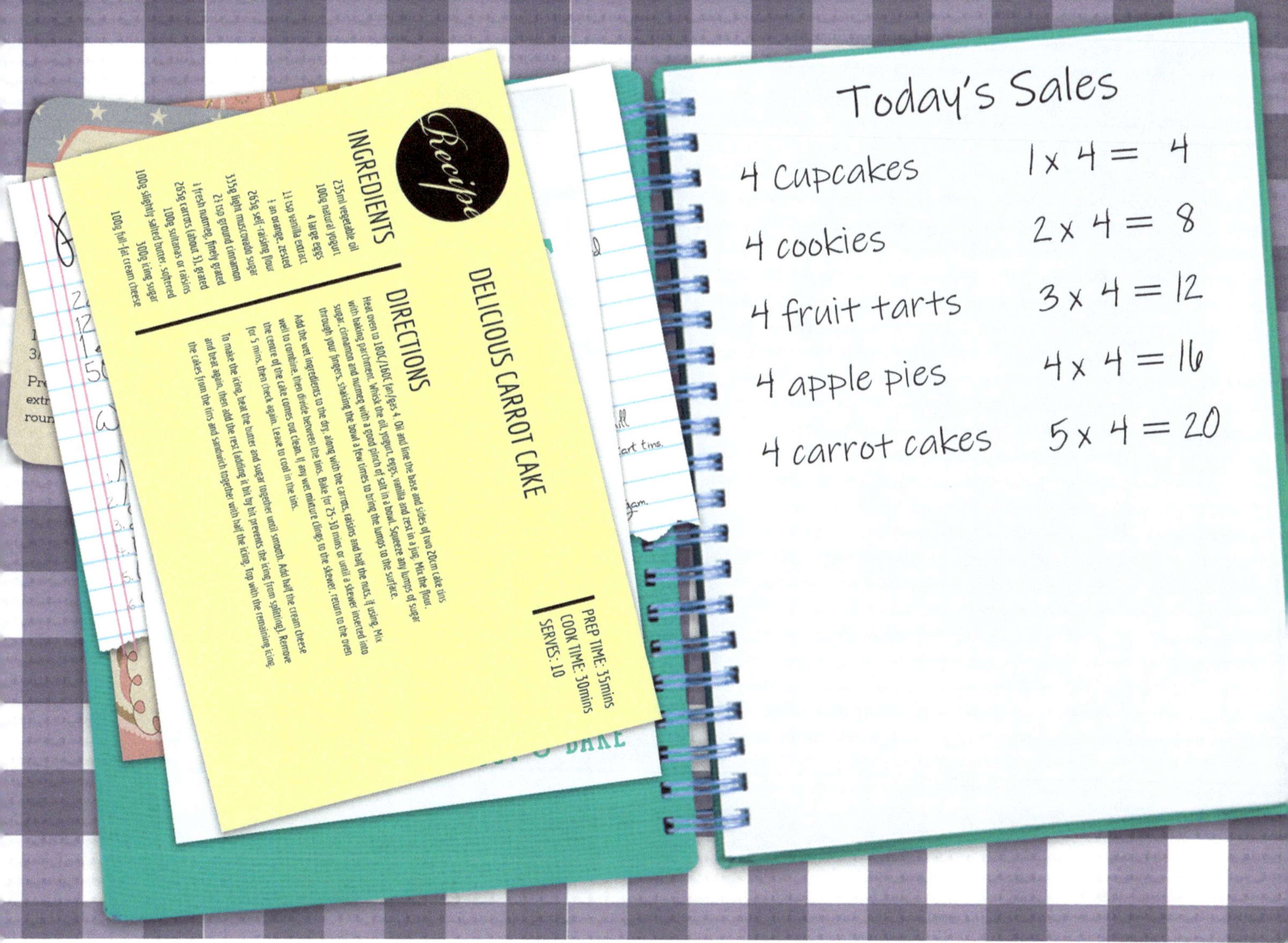

The gardener would like 4 carrot cakes,
those slices are more than plenty.
The baker agrees, pops 4 in a box
and writes 5 x 4 is 20.

It's 1 p.m. and the shop is full
of wonderful goodies to eat.
Ting-a-ling-ling, someone's come in,
wanting to buy a sweet treat.

The florist would like 4 macaroons,
so light, they're what she adores.
The baker beams, pops 4 in a box
and writes 6 x 4 is 24.

It's 2 p.m. and the shop is full
of wonderful goodies to eat.
Ting-a-ling-ling, someone's come in,
wanting to buy a sweet treat.

The musician would like 4 fruit scones but be quick as he's running late*. The baker rushes, pops 4 in a box and writes 7 x 4 is 28.

* What's the fastest cake in the world? Scone!

It's 3 p.m. and the shop is full
of wonderful goodies to eat.
Ting-a-ling-ling, someone's come in,
wanting to buy a sweet treat.

Flapjacks

Ingredients

2 tablespoons (50g) golden syrup

2 tablespoons (50g) butter

8 tablespoons (200g) oats

Method

- Switch oven onto gas mark 5/180 degrees
- In a large saucepan melt the butter on a low heat. Then add the golden syrup and stir. Turn off heat.
- Add oats and stir until the oats are completely coated. You may need to add a little more oats. At this point add any extra ingredients such as chocolate chips, dried fruit, or sweets.
- Tip the mixture onto a greased baking tray and flatten to make sure it is the same thickness. This will ensure it bakes evenly.
- Bake until golden brown. Cut into even squares and lift of baking tray with palate knife.

Today's Sales

4 cupcakes	1 x 4 = 4
4 cookies	2 x 4 = 8
4 fruit tarts	3 x 4 = 12
4 apple pies	4 x 4 = 16
4 carrot cakes	5 x 4 = 20
4 macaroons	6 x 4 = 24
4 fruit scones	7 x 4 = 28
4 flapjacks	8 x 4 = 32

The painter would like 4 flapjacks,
they're syrupy and gooey to chew.
The baker turns, pops 4 in a box
and writes 8 x 4 is 32.

It's 4 p.m. and the shop is full
of wonderful goodies to eat.
Ting-a-ling-ling,
someone's come in,
wanting to buy a sweet treat.

The magician would like 4 blueberry muffins,
as he waits he performs a trick!
The baker claps, pops 4 in a box
and writes 9 x 4 is 36.

It's 5 p.m. and the shop just has
ne plate of goodies to eat.
Ting-a-ling-ling, someone's come in,
wanting to buy a sweet treat.

The clown would like 4 iced buns,
to take back to the circus for tea.
The baker laughs, pops 4 in a box
and writes 10 x 4 is 40.

The window is empty, everything is sold,
everyone has bought their sweet treats.
So come back tomorrow when the window will be full
of wonderful goodies to eat.

1	2	3	4	5	6	7	8	9	10
11	12	13	14	15	16	17	18	19	20
21	22	23	24	25	26	27	28	29	30
31	32	33	34	35	36	37	38	39	40
41	42	43	44	45	46	47	48	49	50
51	52	53	54	55	56	57	58	59	60
61	62	63	64	65	66	67	68	69	70
71	72	73	74	75	76	77	78	79	80
81	82	83	84	85	86	87	88	89	90
91	92	93	94	95	96	97	98	99	100

The numbers in blue show the pattern of the four times table.

What do you notice about the numbers?

Look at the beginning and endings, can you spot a pattern?

1 x 4 = 4

2 x 4 = 8

3 x 4 = 12

4 x 4 = 16

5 x 4 = 20

6 x 4 = 24

7 x 4 = 28

8 x 4 = 32

9 x 4 = 36

10 x 4 = 40

10 and beyond

Times tables don't stop at 10, like they did in the story. They don't stop at 12 either, they go on and on and on - like numbers do, to infinity.

Our number system counts in tens. So, if you know your times tables to 10 then you have all the information you need to go beyond 10 and on and on and on ... Here's how -

If you want to know 12 x 4

$$10 \times 4 = 40$$
$$\underline{\ 2 \times 4 = \ \ 8}$$
$$12 \qquad 48$$

If you want to know 14 x 4

$$10 \times 4 = 40$$
$$\underline{\ 4 \times 4 = \ 16}$$
$$14 \qquad 56$$

If you want to know 20 x 4

$$10 \times 4 = 40$$
$$\underline{10 \times 4 = 40}$$
$$20 \qquad 80$$

Maybe you need to know 36 x 4

$$30 \times 4 = 120$$
$$\underline{\ 6 \times 4 = \ 24}$$
$$36 \qquad 144$$

You might need to know 51 x 4

$$50 \times 4 = 200$$
$$\underline{\ 1 \times 4 = \ \ 4}$$
$$51 \qquad 204$$

How about 74 x 4

$$70 \times 4 = 280$$
$$\underline{\ 4 \times 4 = \ 16}$$
$$74 \qquad 296$$